Etiquette with Angels

Published in 2018 by

David Lovell Publishing
PO Box 44 Kew East
Victoria 3102 Australia
tel/fax +61 3 9859 0000
email publisher@davidlovellpublishing.com

© Copyright 2018 Andrew Bullen SJ

Apart from any fair dealing for the purposes of private study, research, criticism or review, as permitted under the Copyright Act, no part may be reproduced by any process without written permission. Inquiries should be addressed to the publisher.

Front cover image: detail from a woodblock print by Albrecht Dürer, 'The Whore of Babylon', in *The Revelation of St John*, 1498.

Design by David Lovell Publishing
Typeset in 10.5/17 Bernhard Modern
This edition printed through Ingram Spark

National Library of Australia card number
and ISBN 978 1 86355 176 2

Full Cataloguing-in-Publication details available from the National Library of Australia

Acknowledgement
Grateful thanks to the Australian Province of the Society of Jesus for their assistance with the publication of this book.

Etiquette with Angels

Selected and New Poems

ANDREW BULLEN SJ

David Lovell Publishing
Melbourne Australia

A Note from the Author

Music Settings. A number of the poems in this book have been set to music by composer, friend and colleague, Christopher Willcock SJ. These titles are marked with an asterisk*. For further information about Chris Willcock's music and works visit the Australian Music Centre's website, www.australianmusiccentre.com.au.

Dedication

To Kate, Mark and Clare,
in memory of our parents,
Pat and Cliff

Contents

Part 1 Selected Poems

Spiritual	3
Ceremony	4
Imperative	6
Stranger: Just Arrived	7
Etiquette with Angels*	8
Madonna, Child and Parakeet*	10
Gospel Bestiary*	11
Stranger: Beyond Prayer	13
Linguistics	17
One Arrangement of Three Lines	20
O N.Y.!	21
The Return of Persephone	23
How Many Lions?	33
Wisdom*	34
Hospital Notes	35
Minus One	37
Cathay	41
Gibber Country	43
Remembering Isfahan	44
Kreis, Kreis	45

The Demoniac Later	60
Emphasis	62
Sermon to the Birds	63
Speak, Lazarus	64
The Seals	66
Masters of Divinity	67
The Ten Holy Saints of Hartland	69
Mousepoem	79
How the Ocean Is Undermined	81
Exuberance of a Blind Infanta	82
Interior Palomar	83
Pity the Rich	84
Friday 3.30*	85
Naked Runner	86
Mobypoems	88
Laguna de Bay	101
The Buddha of the Southern Ocean	102
Bodhisattva	103
Stone	104
Earth	105
Whingeing Poems	106
Brother Waldmann's Last Carving*	108

Part 2 Recent Poems

The Romans	111
Three Days	112
Epistle to the Welsh	114
Costa Rican Notes	115
Metaphysics/Grammar/Theology	116
Sky-People	117
Prague	120
Jewish Cemetery	121
Kestrel	122
Sparrowpoems	123
So Why Melbourne, Andy?	125

Part 1

Selected Poems

Spiritual

Give me the reticent bravura of dance
    when the music is slow,
    the gestures supple, quick;
let it be sassy, Lord, and statuesque,
    sweaty-tranquil,
and inside itself, like water;
    intent like the body,
    mobile and inventive, and
– spiritual.

Ceremony

All flesh is sorrowful:
music and the pain tell us so.

Without music our pain
is paralysed in mute dismay;

traumatised by memory
flesh and blood can only groan.

From words of pain we wince away,
until the sorrow aches

as music speaks its healing word
to exorcise the pain;

for at the touch of music,
austere yet lambent, our flesh

knows the ache is the pulse of life,
named in tones of sorrow.

But music too, bereft of pain,
is held in rigid trance,

unless a flicker of pain
gives rhythm its human pulse.

How else can music catch
from flesh and blood its plangent theme?

Voicing its pulse of pain
in harmonies of dancing flame,

music sings as if inspired:
all flesh is fire held in time;

for music, when it speaks,
speaks in tongues of fire.

Imperative

There must be silence
for a flower, a word, to grow
singular, prodigious, sacred.

Until flowers and words mutely
explode, attend.

Stranger
"Just arrived"

Just arrived many decades ago:
Customs flashed their Aussie tans
and accents, searched for rotten Pommie fruit.
With nothing to declare, I smuggled in a voice
and set my luggage down in Sydney,
the country's vast arrival lounge
packed with the babble of recent settlers;
brown birds with plastic yellow beaks
gave us cheek; the light, airily strong,
lifted off and landed in all directions.

Etiquette with Angels*

An angel always enters from the left
and keeps its distance from whomever's there.
Through a window a tree may be present;
often the room is opulent and bare.

A vase of flowers is usually placed
between the parties – lilies are preferred.
Dress – informal but not too casual,
for an angel wears simple wings, like a bird.

Late or early, an angel appears on time
(there may be thunder, or a sudden breeze).
However long the wait, you'll be surprised;
without delay, fall humbly to your knees.

Men may gasp, women sigh or drop a book.
The angel speaks first: do not be afraid.
Though itself a message and a miracle,
an angel comes to speak what must be said.

Its words will promise difficult blessings;
so accept them with heartfelt gratitude.
If questions must be asked, keep calm, speak slow,
for an angel fluttered will think you're rude.

Angelic ire can strike you dumb for weeks.
Attune yourself to the music of the spheres;
Whatever cost, keep your guest entertained
without knowing it; be music to pious ears.

Angels never walk away, but vanish
in a golden sky. Never leave before them,
for angels have their special dignity,
and miracles have their own decorum.

Madonna, Child and Parakeet*

A room of sunlight; its marble loggia
double-arched to frame city spires, humped mountains,
the gilded sea – a distant caravel
flutters its pennant, a curlicue of red
across the heavens. A nimbus of stars
crowns the seated girl, burgundy velvet
cloaks the flesh of the holy human forms.
One arm holds snug to her breast the child,
who turns and laughs to see the preening bird
perched on her other hand; its wings shimmer
plumage of crimson and gold: opaline.
All three, madonna, child and parakeet
are poised in sunlight.

An unknown master
painted this some five centuries ago.
Rumour had it, and tired of the girl's slang
and pouting, he half-agrees – she's no virgin;
the child's a writhing bawling brat; the bird
droops in the northern chill, until suddenly,
as if remembering its distant home,
it flexes those brilliant wings, the child,
gurgling with delight, stretches a hand
as if to bless the creature, and the girl too,
pauses, and yields the promise of a smile,
for the room brightens with the gift of sunlight.

Gospel Bestiary*

The lion of Mark ramping on the page
breaks the confines of his uncial cage.

> Perching between the lines in search of food
> fowls of the air peck a beatitude.

> Fishes shoal toward lettering of twine,
> and down the margin tumble herds of swine.

In sacrifice the ox of Luke stamps its hoof
and from men's hearts strikes fire as spoken proof.

> Scorpion and snake we can barely see
> but they lurk in words like "Pharisee".

> While well-fed crowds do basketsful of sums,
> field mice gather for the miracle of crumbs.

The man of Matthew spreads each pinion
to shepherd all beasts into communion.

> Foxes have their holes in open vowels;
> within an inky whale poor Jonah howls.

> The donkey bears through the people's clamour
> his eternal load, and brays "Hosanna".

Without qualm the eagle stares into the sun
where the Johannine word is said and done.

All beasts too receive God's just reward:
goats driven leftward, rightward sheep flock home,
judged by the gold initials of the Lord.

Four loving creatures stand around God's throne,
but far more, both great and small, he calls his own.

Stranger
"This place is beyond prayer"

This place is beyond prayer.
    So at least a glimpse of his scars
(all the remaining leg shrivelled with livid burns)
    revealed to me in a moment of dismay.
I'm used to the mutilations of the other amputees
    and my own I scarcely notice;
but his scars took my breath away,
    provoked the need to stare.
The others too, more or less at ease
    with being figures mutilated
for the judgment of the unscarred,
    know he stood like judgment among us;
our faces told each other: we've never seen
    anything so bad; look again.

We obey the courtesies: leave each other alone,
    make room, offer talk: "In for repairs ..."
"Getting a new one", "Busy place, the Repat",
    'How long since yours?", "Cancer, as a child",
"Seven operations I've had; they buggered me up;
    bush doctors they were."
The physio says, "Swing your hips more, Mr Smith."

The flesh is criss-crossed where the tyres ate in
    (make yourself look) skin like wax trickling under flame;
he moves among us, as we move ourselves:
    ungainly, nonchalant, bold,
pretending to be as normal
    as we know we are.

A young brickie (his triceps bulge as he swings on his crutches,
    his torso trim and hard) says, "My girl calls these stump-
        socks
doodle-bags"; there's laughter here of course. Momentarily
    a face will wince, more with discomfort than pain,
as if touched by the agitations of fire.
    A dapper gentleman with a clipped moustache
gently keeps his reserve. Next to him, a bikie,
    a leg of his jeans empty, reads westerns all afternoon.
"Watch out, I'm going to kick for goal": another old joker,
    taking careful aim along the bars, watched by his fussing
        son.
A few soldiers, sometimes a wino, refugees, farmers:
    these are the old; the young come from accidents or
    disease.
We know we've been tested, tried by fire;
    can say at times we've thrived,
know at least we've survived;
    if proud, we know the cost of pride.

"The wet weather on the farm gets at the leather,
    here, inside the limb, and rots it."
The technicians alone are told our secrets: "It hurts here"
    (tailors to our aches and pains). "That bolt's not
        touching?"
"Balance OK?" "We'll tighten the straps more."
    Then a hugely fat man enters, voice dominating
        the room,
hooting with jollity: "Hope there are no women present,
    I've left my jocks at home." But he too can be caught

pausing, the face in a momentary trance
    wondering what has happened, surprised again
by the shock that never goes.
    We flinch to touch the scar
we touch a thousand times without a thought.
    Once, I remember, my hand ached to touch
curved and shining musculature of ancient stone:
    "Torso Belvedere: Do Not Touch",
a fragment greater than the whole,
    showing to Michelangelo in pitted marble
the anatomy of the divine.
    But we flinch from what's carved in human flesh,
see there only cicatrices of pain.
    The body is the sacrament of the self.

"Any trouble with the phantom pains?"
    Not pains really, more like threads of memory,
ticklish, half-numb.
                How his flesh was pared down,
    chiselled on a turning lathe, then years of burnishing.
Lines from another place come to mind:
    On your loom of timeless fire, weave, craftsman,
    your strands of pain into an ancient harmony.

The talk has faded; we turn to last month's magazines;
    yawn; try out new or mended limbs. Surviving the
    carnage,
the mayhem, the survivors walk in fire.
    There's no need to say, *"Noli me tangere";*
you cannot reach us here, only join us.
    Only within the fire do we reach other.

If God is here, he's here on our terms:
    walk with us in the burning fiery furnace,
few notice, and here it doesn't matter.
    That flesh of his is wood rotted,
corroded bronze.
    It's time to introduce ourselves,
as we say goodbye, shake hands.

Linguistics

1.
Ludwig Wittgenstein, we have need of you:
help us chart the meaning and seek the true;
since abstraction is no ecstasy of thought,
we'll read between the silences as you taught;
show us, cartographer, urban and urbane,
language is only human, almost humane.

2.
You cannot use the same language twice:
the river flows; a frozen river is no use.

Each day insurrection breaks out
in the arcaded piazzas of the ancient city,
reverberates through the neat suburbs
to echo, dwindle, in the surrounding foothills;
but always, up there, in the cordilleras
silence, hiding its own forbidden city:
call it, for want of a proper name,
Lhasa, Shangri-La, New Jerusalem.

3.
The history of silence
is never broken;
always, somewhere, a voice
stays attentive to how quiet
each word can be.

Since all speech is provisional,
even poetry,
the silence we can never disrupt
we await.

4.
The spoken universe of things remained
unknown before naming Adam
mastered each gift with sound
belonging to the namer and the named:
star, beast, fowl, tree, hand, snake.
So it was he heard the silence underlined
and found himself alone.
Asleep, he dreamed a new way of speaking;
awake, and speaking, he found an answering voice:
"Your voice calling answered me."
They sang the harmonies of flesh,
and found themselves alone,
surrounded by the distant stars.
The wordy snake within the unknown tree
gave breaking promises.
So Adam ate his words.

5.
Think of voices beyond language
but before silence,
like, say, hrrmph, tut-tut, clunk,
oh, aargh, oo, hey-ho, ugh!
whoopee, oi, ah-ha, or ha

– the sounds we make in play,
    or love (whoops),
    or war (whoops again),
    in song too;
foreigners use them
for language – imagine Japanese,
the lingo of anthropophagi,
Caliban on his island
and Ariel everywhere,
the cooing of birds;
none of these speak as we do
but somewhere else.

6.
Birds in flight at dusk
    come to the delta
– among the reeds
    voices indistinct, reciprocal:
if not human, then perhaps the birds themselves
    wailing or singing,
or the river's own murmur
    "I am the river that drowns in your sea",
and the remote reply
    "Come to me, hard river";
if not language, then whole sounds
    – hieroglyphs perhaps;
at least the cry of ibis to the orange moon
    desolate above the reeds.

One Arrangement of Three Lines

poems broadcast
silence
in various languages

O N.Y.!

The moon, as if eyeing a near-equal, eyes
New York.
The people here are melting
into New Yorkers, and maybe Americans,
maybe citizens of the good ole U S of A,
denizens, certainly, of Long Island, of Manhattan.
I woke up in the middle of the night saying
Yew Nork, Yew Nork.
Arrogance can be forgiven of a people
who live in a dump
like New Jersey.
There are no apples
in New York.
Magical people lived here: Jackie O., O Willem
de Kooning, Mstislav Rostropovich,
Orphan Annie, Woody Allen and
1,000,000s more
in O New York.
While you read this someone
is murdered in New York
by a New Yorker.
Its many bridges are all of them beautiful,
spectral, and mooring New York
to America;
one night, glittering, it will sail away.
The most distinctive features of the Bronx
are its name and a zooful of New Yorkers.

The sax and the klax
are the music of New York:
Newyorkophones.
The deaf alone can always see it
as beautiful: tower after tower
of lighted space,
each with its own distant purpose.
Superman was truly at home here
and O Lois Lane; it suited King Kong too.
The most important place
in New York
is where the skyscrapers join the ground
or leave it.
Inhabited by other countries
(Brooklyn has its own language)
it is more than equal to the rest
of America;
it keeps Chicago in its place.
Except for the Guggenheim
you never see the inside;
New York is all outside,
a badly eroded mountain range
other people have built.
The Chrysler Building, silvery
and cinematic, is the most beautiful thing
in New York
(and indeed America);
it makes New York
New York.
As you've guessed
I've never been there.

The Return of Persephone

                    Imagine your island.
This is mine:
    the light rises sheer out of the ground,
even the dark the four cypresses possess shimmers;
beyond, cicadas drill-drill the arid air;
nearer, the slender sway of eucalypt,
clumps of lavender, rosemary, press their scent
through the open shutters into blue shadows
– a quiet place now my friends have left.
Earthenware jug and basin, wicker chair,
the closed third room, are mine again. "Why go?
This is the first day of heat", and at the harbour
"Don't write." Then – still using finger-language –
I bought bread, olives, a small red fish
and took an hour to stroll back from the village.
Already the ferry moves beyond the other islands
towards Piraeus. Islands haunt the horizon,
each with its own god or goddess, and saints,
its fame for wine or quarry or ruins,
or a statue the pride of some foreign museum;
they had their own coins too. The sea surges its murmurs
below the cliff crumbling beyond the citrus grove;
on a trestle near the verandah but out in the sun
a spiral of orange peel and a glass of water,
cold and pure, the house a dazzling cube behind;
the heat strokes the sweat out of my back
as I finger a grain-knot in this silky timber,
touch the glass. The world is pungent
and my heart is easy; I find myself murmuring

    "the return of Persephone",
a poem imposes itself,
  everything has a rind,
"she brought - no, she brings the darkness with her",
  everything has a core.

What does it mean, "the return of Persephone"?
This is what I think:
  each spring my body comes back to me,
but this year more than ever. Why?
— *nescio*, but I wanted/needed to read the Odyssey again,
desperately borrowed Charlie's copy, and Aeschylus,
and most of Sophocles, and Seferis again,
and my body was returning all the time.
  One quiet afternoon
the cypresses in the garden I saw as green thunderbolts,
and tried to remember the Greek word for "thunderbolt"
— I still can't; it begins with zed.
  I plundered the library:
Greek myths, Greek art, Greek poems, travel guides to
  Greece,
"Who is Persephone? And Demeter, who is she?"
  I remembered how, at fourteen, returning to London
from Africa with Kate, we landed at Athens;
but she was sick and I missed everything, even the Acropolis;
there were clouds of dust at the airport, and oily fried eggs
and my anger.
  I recalled the Victorian encyclopedia
with its engravings of Greek divinities — pudgy, jowly, noble
and Victorian, a gilt-edged book, heavy and repulsive.
  I collected Greek epithets:

the sea – wine-dark, of course, and dolphin-torn,
    gong-tormented,
snot-green and scrotum-tightening, and had my own
dolphin blue-grey. Useless.
    I remembered Keats imagining himself in the trenches
shouting with Achilles. Marvellous.
    I gathered Greek words
in English, such as Australian plants – eucalypt, melaleuca.
    I thought of light and John's Gospel,
and tried reading the New Testament in Greek.
    I was struck by the singularity of each thing.
    I found myself saying "I have never been to Greece;
no need, my body lives there."
(I was living an inarticulate myth.)
    I was wondering how Europe could suddenly appear
like this in Australia, and how there congregated around
    Persephone
disparate phrases:
"Victory assured, the goddess bends
to loosen her sandal."
        "Freud is never far away."
        "Jung, though, is closer."

"The women are laughing,
the men are beautiful,
their faces know
their strength must fade."
        "Did she think the worst of darkness over?"
"What men or gods these? What maidens loth?"
        "About her lips the promise of smile".
I had many ideas about this poem,

but little idea how to control it. I discovered how it will end,
and how it will begin:
    "Imagine your island. This is my island."
And then I waited.

The island doesn't matter
– a device to edge us into Greece
and towards two phrases,
a context, familiar and alien,
plausible and perhaps too narrow.
Ignore the island.

Some of this poem is fact,
all of it is fiction.
Since the island is part of the poem
the island is true,
a device to translate us somewhere else
so that we may go further to somewhere else again.

Why should Persephone resurface here?
So far from Europe,
where we want to be antipodean in every way;
laconic and ironic, yes, and supposedly egalitarian.
positivist, wary of the antique, eager for the future?
How can we recover her ancient form?

An ode to Persephone?
You move over the meadow like a breeze.
    This is your homecoming; rejoicing earth
Greets your return each spring with budding trees,
    The wild iris announces your rebirth
In whispers the bright echoes of the leaves

Declare and fruit enlarge with golden yells.
Released from darkness you bring sudden dawn,
  Your mother no longer grieves,
For the cold of winter your cry dispels.
  Her laughter is the laughter of the corn.

In gusts, flower-scented, you greet each other;
  Your mingling tears voice wonder and delight,
Ended now the journeys of the mother,
  Returned again her days narcissus-bright.
Hearing such voices, his heart proving true,
  Mankind performs the rights of gratitude:
"Your mother's laughter ripens our human corn;
  You bring the darkness with you
That our vines and olives may be renewed;
  Receive these fruit, this wine, this lamb newly-born."

Goddess, you are the troubled messenger
  Between the forceful dark and gentle light.
Your mother's embrace subdues your terror
  Who were husbanded by the power of night.
You bring her tribute from the dead anew
  To nourish our harvest. Bright-berried olives
You yield, yet grasp still the pomegranate
    – O take the brightness with you
If you desire the smiling dark …
      . . . .

[Imagine the rest is missing.]
Make what you can of these poemshards:
          "your lover, rich in dead",
"you are sown in the dark",
          "do you miss the dark one?"

What use to us a broken amphora,
an artifact too beautiful,
its shape beyond our needs,
seeming Greek, but Romantic and English?
Even if the antique form freezes
the most telling moment into sculpture
– and how difficult to move the story
from gesture to stony gesture –
how can it be more than exotic ornament
among the freshness of scrub and eucalypt?

The myths make nature personal.
We are far from them.
There is no Persephone;
she too is a contrivance:
forget Persephone.

Maybe we can abandon ourselves,
journey towards her world
with our own speech.
Maybe we can be half-haunted
by her language roughly transformed:
the Homeric hymn tells how she was snatched away
from the world of flowers
to which each year she returns to turn away again.

Let me sing of Demeter, the corn-haired one,
And her slender-ankled daughter, Persephone:
Thunder gave her to Darkness. Her father, Zeus,
Watches everything but let her be taken.
She was laughing with the Daughters of the Sea
(Their robes ripple wave-like), and far from her mother,

The giver of golden fruit. In the meadow
They gathered sweet flowers: rose, crocus, violet,
Iris, hyacinth, and then a bright flower,
Never seen before, grown to entice the maiden
(Shy as a doe): narcissus, a star earth-bound,
So bright all who saw it laughed in quick wonder,
The immortal gods as much as mortal man.
For the girl too the earth was more beautiful,
So she stretched out both hands to pluck the flower.
But wide-pathed earth gaped in the plain of Nysa;
The Dark One, who receives all at last, leapt up,
Snatched her away. She cried out to the God
Who gives all gifts. But no god nor mortal man
Heard her voice, nor did the bright-berried olives.

We have heard her story but not her voice.
Travel to meet her, on her island, in her sacred grove.
Try to forget the journey we have made,
pretend to forget our language and use hers:

Δήμητρ' ἠύκομον, σεμνὴν θεόν, ἄρχομ' ἀείδειν,
αὐτὴν ἠδὲ θύγατρα τανύσφυρον, ἣν Ἀιδωνεὺς
ἥρπαξεν, …

Even these strange sounds tangled on our lips
cannot sound her silences,
and always always reveal the journey we have made.
We have lost her music.

She comes, sudden as dream-visitor,
as if darkness rises sheer out of the ground.
A phrase from nowhere

– "she brings the darkness with her" –
must come from somewhere.
Jung is never far away.
The life we are conscious of
is not the life we lead.

Maybe the death of someone
made the dark flower bloom again
inside me.
"Darkness" is on my tongue.

She is older than her myth,
her face is not marble,
not even a mask of golden foil,
but more enduring, undiscovered.
So she persists,
and must speak freely
as if she naturally has our voice.

In the woods lives a goddess,
many-named, chameleon-voiced,
vivid as oranges. Standing before you
sheer as light, the goddess speaks,
there are tears in her voice,
she is bereft of music:
"We meet in the world, I salute you.
My husband is rich in dead.
I, who was snatched by darkness,
darkness lay with me, care for them.
We remember the shadow of each other's life.
The worst of darkness is over,
your body always remembers me.

*I greet the dead as they come to me,
I shall greet you,
befriend me, receive your freedom."*

Remember the island:
    Somewhere offshore, the rumours say, is a drowned ship,
lost moving westward, its freight: amphorae of wine,
dyed-cloths, pottery, coins, knick-knacks, two statues.
A diver plunges again and again for sponges into the naked
    sea.
You are that diver.
A futile dive, your knife lost,
breathless you kick at the sand to rise,
look at the quicksilver surface,
your foot scrapes something hard – a curlicue of blood,
you glance down at the patina of a woman's face,
soar upward, shout into the gasping air
"a statue, a statue".
It is the mask of Persephone,
about her lips the promise of a smile.
You bring the darkness with you.

Here the gum leaves are always falling
and new leaves replace them,
as if the seasons never come and go
but only stay,
as if my body is living and dying
all the time,
as if the darkness rising out of the ground
brought the brightness with it,
and Persephone's voice mingled terror and delight.

Words, like tackle, haul her toward the quicksilver light,
the sand streams from the folds of her robe.
The naked men stand clear,
the women observe her antique smile.
All know their strength must fade
but realise their bodies are figures of myth:
the women are laughing, the men are beautiful.

Words, like stones, are gathered and ordered,
other orderings are possible,
the gathering is incomplete.
There are left-over fragments:
              "my body is all Greek to me",
"you were abandoned to darkness by your father,
you were tempted by his gift".

A metope from a ruined temple,
its pieces dispersed through foreign lands:
          Two women like goddesses,
               the fall of their tunics
                    stirred by a marble breeze,
      stand face to face
            in tears of greeting and farewell.

This is my poem.
          Imagine yours.

How Many Lions?

With book after book of God's Word
the cave's a tight fit
without a lion underfoot.
The old bare scholar, irascible,
kicks out at space, at a skull
lying there, at so many
many words – ancient, holy,
untranslatable into Latin vulgarity;
but always carefully he edges past
the imperturbable beast
which keeps its counsel
and stays in the way.
Sometimes the lion licks his hand:
the saint sits to his task,
inches his way
line by line through the Testaments;
meanwhile, the lion is a lion.

Wisdom*

Caspar, Caspar, do not be afraid
of me, of yourself, and even of Herod.

Do not fear that Melchior and Balthazar
will doubt your story, or be jealous
that I came to you alone.
If they claim that you are young,
or black, or dream too much,
admit it.
    Make them remember
how they felt when Herod smiled.
You all trusted his welcome.
Notice how you shudder now
at his innocent request.

The child needs no other homage
than that of the riff-raff shepherds,
yourselves with your silly gifts,
the heavens singing or your shifting star,
the warm breath of ox and ass,
Joseph's vigilance and the arms of Mary.

You cannot prevent the slaughter.
Arise and disobey the king.

Hospital Notes

Quiet Please

Quiet please,
they are switching off
life-support switches;
whatever remains is medical – orderly;
the clean sheets cover
a white space, and murmurs
will soon become speech again.

Time to Go

So we turned away
from him, knowing all
was said. How are you feeling?
Trouble is, I'm not feeling.
Though half-grateful
we came, he was tired
of us, and himself and waiting,
so said goodbye for good.

Soft Tissue

The soft noises and sweet nurses
will be dreadful –
plastic tubes leave and enter
me – my skin is soft tissue –
sunlight on a broken wall
merely sunlight –

small gestures, say, to smooth and pluck
the edge of a sheet, and habitual wryness
turned, with late visitors there,
against myself – at a loose end –
ready for night shift –
the last visitor stainless
steel, wingless. If I'm lucky, that is.

Minus One

Blessing

With a sense of balance
better than any biped's,
I'd better start counting
my blessings: minus one.

Resurrection

Some years ago after weeks
of quiet and prayer the pain
I had totally forgotten
came back. O yes, Mum said,
you had pain. I buried it
deep in my body,
until my body suddenly remembered the weight
of it. The body forgets nothing
and will say, loosened by weeks
of quiet and prayer perhaps,
pick up yourself and walk.

Cliché

Reliving how when
just thirteen and not knowing
it was cancer
delirious believing
I was dying panic
fast-forward dark blossoming

fountain at my heart and quailing
I don't want to die Mummy
Daddy I don't (still don't)
the dark bud's there still
am still dying and know
nobody who is not so
and know it'll break out.

Greetings
Waking up minus a leg
the night nurse beside me,
she was new and never seen again
and serene, and she said
quietly happy birthday.

Thirteen
It was a lovely autumn,
the Rome Olympics were running,
my birthday was soon: would you like
a dog? Yes O yes, a dachshund
please, just like the one we saw.
Jack wants you to visit them
in Africa. Why was I being given
so much to live for? That evening
on the day before the day before
with Dad at the foot of the bed
just before Mum told me,
I guessed.

Patient

Dad said, tomorrow you can start getting better,
years later people said, you're looking better,
nowadays, how well you're looking,
back in Wales I knocked on Dr Antony's door
to say, here's one of your successful patients
after all these years. He said,
you're looking very well.

Suntan

The nurse I bantered with over
who had the better suntan
(her card said from the nurse
who's browner than you) said
pulling away the iodine bandage
they've done a good job, what a lovely wound.
It is so still.

Treasure

Life as a local charity
I took to: my stamp collection
doubled with old Dr Lee's penny reds,
pages of Bundespost, the '37 Coronation set;
thruppences, sixpences, shillings collected
at school for me burst their bags
all over me, showered, tinkled across the fireplace.
Now the stamps are stored somewhere.
That ordinary generosity though I treasure.

Phantom

The nerve ends transmit
for many decades the last message:
the leg is there; which is false.
The instep, the small toe, the upper calf,
back of the bent knee – O now almost all the foot –
the outer thigh – just soft pins and needles;
curiosity, amazement, everything's OK,
nothing is there except the feeling.

The court of heaven

Mr Toby James, my surgeon, spoke.
The residents hovered round him as
he and I conversed as if only he and I
knew what was happening
and they were there to learn
by overhearing. Everybody wore white.

The nurses pulled away the browny gauze
to praise his handiwork.
"Mr Toby James
has done a marvellous job. Andrew look –
what a lovely scar."
I am still proud to say.

Cathay

Recall that traveller, Matteo Ricci,
seeking always in the secret faces
and the old-fangled words a new calligraphy
that rumours hope of the heart's Cathay.

Imagine him pausing in the warm damp air
to watch a flight of cormorants
fold themselves into the brown waters,
wondering how he will ever learn to learn
the familiar gestures of the crowd,
to ignore the haze of noise,
to forget Matteo Ricci; and marvelling
that he must be a cosmographer
to tell cosmographers of a sad man on a cross,
and deft master of their ancestral truths
to prove his master theirs; and catching himself
praying from the middle kingdom of his heart.

Like him, be a pilgrim: the most distant languages and people
are holy places; and know that he discovered himself
no longer Matteo Ricci but Li Ma-tou;
find, like him, at last our barbarian God
in the mandarin silence.

Gibber Country

thehorizonflatandredthreatenswithitsmonotonousblur,unless gibber stones
reveal the land is delicate   is red stones   stones moss furred stones
      an ochre pebble   a pebble streaked with ochre
a pebble mottled ochre and quartz   sandstone wedge   khaki bush
        desert foam   bush   a lizard trim nimble and green
      scimitar and spikes of leaves   each tuft of grass
hills tawny as lions crouching   palisades of peppermint bark
      palaver of foliage   fernspray   cloud flocks nibbling blue pasture
        hills looping violets   pin down gorse
      green/gold tones shift under gauze of blossom
        saplings stand in thousands   a currawong gargles
fallen branch haunches   a bronze fly buzzes / settles / probes
      scribble gum   black stubble   gum scribble
              birds alert and clear/cut
      that pride of hills behind   a sudden rise of furze
        lakewater like milk rippling   a blue heron
                                                tiptoes
        pearl ripples   the creek smuggling clouds aloft
                                                into its blue
  and water seawards   look! the usual gifts of spring/silence
            a moorhen squeaks on its hinges
strands of willow patterns
here and there a human voice, like a pebble
      the scalloped bay
        below   pottery cliffs: sea ware
      sea skeins at dusk   sifted sand   red grains   pearly grains
    sand shifted   a grain of sand: a red pearl
        a lavender shell (the shape of australia) purple stipple
the last smudge of day now under each star   gibber stars
        shining gibber country
we should be a subtle people, our speech almost gibberish

Remembering Isfahan

We came in tears along the Silken Road
    from Samarkand. Our wounds gaped fearfully;
mine, so we thought, were fatal. Riderless,
    the Prince's horse fretted for his master;
at Isfahan, by the gate, an old man
    fingered the blood on the saddle and cried
"Him too they have blinded", but the sentry
    only murmured "From Samarkand in flames."
Our haste was the news we brought, clattering
    through the darkened echoes of the city;
but already in the mountains thunder
    from their drums sparked such panic among us
that our libraries were put to the torch.
Halting at last before the Turquoise Mosque,
    we stilled our sovereign's bewildered prayers;
but in my fever I could only gaze
    on the stillness of the shimmering dome
below an icy moon, until, in rain,
    the characters of the Sacred Name dissolved.
When the surgeons had done with me, my friend,
    with a glance at the deserted foothills,
could only say, "There is a futile task
    I have to do." We touched each other's hands
in parting. He spoke again: "Some will survive,
    but this is the end of everything."

Kreis, Kreis

(La chevauchée de la discorde)
Know the soundless galloping
of the horse and the rider of discord:
the horse, half ant-eater in mid-air

leaps over its own shadow on the landscape;
the rider holds a torch of woolly fire
and fingers the terrible details of its sword.

Autumn leaves bloat to vast clouds,
the usual visionary trees are blasted,
black flowers stand on the other side.

The violence and the blood are done as careful
as the work of crows; the bodies, routed,
are piled orderly and ready us for later.

(Not Schönbrunn)
Note how well-ordered, clean,
the place is: the trees flourish,
the birds sing: how the sun shines

on whitewash; note the suburban industrial chimneys
work nearby, and "Do not write on walls"
is posted up in various languages;

how waterplants in the beautiful brook
sway like green hair and the main courtyard
opens up its proportions like Schönbrunn's.

Note how at the memorial two gardeners measure
the distance between   marigold   marigold   marigold
with a ruler; on the wall by the three incinerators

and the beam with the three hanging hooks
is a washbasin. Note how tidy, anal,
hell is and how it works.

(Leap Up Darkness)
The way it can leap up suddenly darkness
saying, say, drown yourself, let yourself drown,
or crash the car, crash it.

Revulsion yes but impulse too to fascination
and then knowledge heartfelt: this is me, this me
in need of saving; and observe all this coolly.

(Small Details)
Violence to work must be quiet
and ordinary, implacable and like the crack
of linen sharply shook out.

The people must be kept/pushed away
and made to sweat to hear the sound
in the middle of the night of the lift come clank-clanking up.

It can be seen in small details
like a crush of eggshells
piled high and feathery against a pane of glass;

in photos of atrocities the way men's corpses
so often have shirts shoved upwards
exposing their bellies/privates.

It can suddenly swing on you in dreams like when
a door pushed open into sloshing rain releases
swaying from a pulley a damp weighted sack

or a body that swings close
to thud and thud against the soaked door
and show its face as your face.

(Labyrinth)

The only way out is down,
the only way out is further in,
the straightest way out is round and round.

Let no one but a little child lead you,
who carries a light and the other hand holds your hand,
the only way out is down.

Do not expect or hunger to see the worst,
you will see enough, others can bear more,
the only way out is further in.

If you become like a child you can
get out of here, past the damned, their horses/beasts, the lost,
the straightest way out is round and round.

The only way out is further in,
the only way out is down,
you too are the minotaur.

(A Creature of Habit)
"The place had its attractions
for a creature of habit, the conditions
suited me and the job had to be done.

I miss the times when we injected.
When will the doctor return
for the experiments? Let me
show you around around

but keep out of my space. I liked
it here, it gave my talents
scope. We are out of syringes

but there are rooms and rooms full
of hair, shoes, spectacles: ready for use.
Any weather, rain or shine,

was time enough for the job.
Now there's nothing doing.
Women had a hand in this too you know;

they too like to smash things and clean them up.
Look how the square is hosed down spotless and empty
of human muck."

(Entrance)
Imagine how it was when
the sky was not this blue
but with plumes of black tumescing,

nor was the transport, crowded already,
driven by our jolly driver, who called out
"Who wants the camp? Jump aboard",

nor did they enter the entrance free,
but were shunted here: rubbish down the drain,
shit to the sewers, ditched.

(Circling)

Once inside the girl said, "My country is a sad place,
I'm from Cape Town", but said no more about it,
besides this was no place for that. "May I stay near you

as I walk around this place?" It would be wrong to say no.
This was no place to be alone. I told her nothing about myself.
We walked around touching nothing, noting trivia,

the pretty stream for example. How many people died here?
Thousands, many thousands. This was one of the smaller
places and most of the victims were Germans themselves.

Holding back from touching anything, from imagining,
from being swamped or the heart blowing out,
noting for later, years later,

the way reading the paper your eye skims
across the atrocities in other countries
or your own to the literary section or sport.

There was gravel, small stones, underfoot everywhere.
Who besides Dante and the damned
enters hell wittingly?

(Close-Up)
The mirror shows my own fallen-angel face
ice-hard, nice, keep-away face,
push-away, punch-out-at, ready-to-spit-out-at face,

a "nothing there" looking back face,
a "no you" hell-better-than-heaven, well-guarded by its own
    emptiness,
face, itself an iron helmet closed-up face: face it.

(Inside the Demons)
We circle within (wet night glistened)
circling circles (and dried on the concrete yard
vast and empty) on our treadmill patrol.

Guards' names and numbers had listed mine.
One rose up (helmeted) before me
with a fallen angel face, his eyes barbed wire.

He whistled cold hard blasphemies and said
"Who brought you here, or did you come
of your own accord?" (Unanswered) so he laughed

"You're one of us in disguise. Names are nuisances,
numbers work better, and now this place is cleaned up,
I keep on guard to keep it so. Walk with me."

So we dreamwalk(ed) around and around. He said
"My skin is iron-hard, but inside I'm frightened, lonely,
cold, but inside again relish violence

and so want to thrill at (know) how blood blossoms,
the welcome scream, the randy crunch of bones,
kill by numbers, (a blunt knife snags on itself).

So "give-and-take", "be gentle" is nausea, stomach
lurches at subhuman (*untermenschlich*) frailty.
For goodness' sake for the devil's sake, patrol yourself."

(Internal Bruising)

Many years ago I spent a morning walking in hell.
The city train glided out to Dachau,
the suburban bus dropped us at the gate.

Inside was spotless and the Carmel nearby
in silence, as we all were. I walked around the place
once, with a girl who did not want to do it alone,

and returned to Munich with an obscene, crazy
New Yorker. It has been inside me
ever since, waiting; it was there before

as prayer had shown and telling me to go there.
This was no place to enter alone and who
was my guide? I still do not know.

Edith Stein, was it? And yes, I've read Dante since.
My ordinary life and teaching children has gone on but
I have been a long way out of myself,

and feelings have only dared come held by words
and the undertone everywhere of *eleison*,
eleison, alas, alas, enough, enough.

The circles were inevitable, and I found
some of heaven and all of hell
were the same place with love accepted or rejected;

either way our flesh is scorched:
arms spread to open the breast to rainfire,
or turned back bent, huddled.

I have not wept; maybe words are tears
another way, or internal bleeding/bruising,
but I have not felt it enough I know.

As long as this calm, my happiness and laughter
are not indifference; and maybe I'm held almost still
in the incoming tide of silence, numbed and vast.

(Alas, Alas)
The sacrifice of children goes on and on,
the playgrounds are emptied of laughter,
the old idols and the new keep up their hunger.

The snake loops and loops itself around the nest,
(yet the ghetto children dance until they drop),
a new age flounders into its own bloodshed,

and the old reign/regime of terror attacks, attacks
before the child awakes: the curriculum of hatred
is drunk in with mother's milk.

The last dauphin (or czarevitch), every beggar's child,
is ground down by our turning and turning millstones;
worse is getting them to poison/abuse themselves and each other.

When they laugh, it falls on us like rainfire;
as we bruise the bud, we bewail the loss, the loss.
Worst is the death of their eyes.

(Wrench)

The deepest pain is seismic; the pressed-
hardest pressure on/through muscle; subdued fire
along the seam where a scar joins; or a pain ridge

reawakening and then the pain: or not the pain in it
but the shock: this is happening to me, like the red
shock of blood or quick probing firewires,

and the time long, oh so long, and tired, so tired,
like a tree weighted with so many leaves, tries to let them go.
I mean the wrenching spiral in bone core.

(Jabber, Jabber)

Wassat behold bright beastie of the air?
A vulpire curdling overdead the faminlies,
forceman of the shocktrips, so violet is choler?

Moan outgraves. Wrath is it munschling the kindlies?
By war, by war, hangered its gassly idol smile.
In this jabberlabberrink don't all kindlings dumble?

Can you decry hear comes the tickticktockodile,
inferno-red its playgueful more? Feefiefofumble
the booglieman wants to prey his rattletattoo.

Come pale horse, its raider Death. O how hellig this.
Mein himmler! behound him! atishoo achtungshoo
we all foul down, wassat smell? hear/look   owch/hisss.

(Nadezhda)
Also, beyond O way way beyond
the eastern marches hope was abandoned
and then hope against hope struggled, survived

on heart-learnt poems, a scanty diet
to hold off starving and give courage to scream out against
terror, exile, enforced silence: and so be human.

(Slow Motion, Slow)
I was squatting on the ground, surrounded
by all my slight victims – all squatting around me
and saying nothing into the brown air.

Then one whose deformed ear I (a child) had slapped
– my skills in brutality were learnt in childhood –
arose and said nothing, but stepped into

my space. I said "I have no need of you,
out you go", and shoved him away,
but he returned and returned.

One by one each victim stood, did not accuse
but said (simply) what I had done, stood there
and then crouched down. They gathered around

like friends, children. I heaved myself up
to heave, shunt them out, I wanted cleared
cleaned my own space, so shoved

battered them away/out. Hour after hour
they returned, reached towards me
until exhausted I slumped down

against a tree. "What are you doing?"
a voice whispered, "Where is your brother?"
"I have no brother, want none", but asked

"And how did you, small voice, come here:
were you brought, or come by yourself?"
He replied so quietly, "Both."

"And why?" "How else could I reach you
other than by being one/all of your victims?"
Suffering dribbled from his mouth.

He was strapped to the blood-streaked tree
that stood at the centre of my space.
I staggered up to stand

my ground. He would not budge,
was too strong for me. "I" collapsed
for me and became the circle of my victims.

(Enough, Enough)
The day and night trains, eastwards day and night,
did not relent, the deciders between death, death, life, death
did not relent, nor the guards, nor the corpse-sorters,

nor the never-ending fires and towers of smoke
reaching up to heaven (did not relent), although it is only human
to break the circle, to relent, to break away,

although the burial of the dead never ends,
and Rachel always weeps for her children,
it is only human to step back (a step or two)

turn away, leave the place of sorrow,
as the three Maries left the sealed tomb,
Dante leaves each circle, a poem ends, enough, enough.

(Meaning)
Where has the darkness come from
rising inside like a henge of stone black
crematorium smoke billowing up?

Am I blind or what, not
to notice the cause, with, after all,
only my tiny will the source, is it?

And yet threatens to cover everything,
a pillar of death by day,
and all of night by night.

(Ravens, Ravens)
I heard two birds nattering: the old one said
"Go for the soft parts, the paler flesh."
– "O why, why?" crowed the other.

"To get at the rest easier, my young friend.
Learn from the past: clean up the eyes."
– "They glitter and hide", the other cried.

"With your black and shiny tent-like wings
cover what you are doing. Go for the lights."
– "Nowadays, you old ones say, the supply is never-ending."

"Before it was mostly battles and famine.
Ruffle up your courage. Keep tapping
on the bone, go for the marrow.

Peck on, peck hard, before they dry out
and leathery, my carrion friend." – "Yes, yes", the youngster
    cawed,
"O let us assert ourselves at the human feast."

(East)
*"Ich fahre in den Osten, wo die Sonne
aufgeht."* East-bound, yes, but the train shrieked,
the door slammed and she vanished for ever.

Its rhythms jolted until they slid,
for the trains to hell run on time
clickety-click, clickety-click, clickety-

click. She had written and prayed in her cell to explain/
receive anything that might happen before it did.
Her chosen sisters years later keep their mouths shut

on silence nearby. She meant: to go back,
to enter hell if necessary, to be shunted east, is
to ascend. As if to say, my place

is to be with my chosen people wherever they are
crowded, kraaled, laagered, encamped,
stripped of everything, fumigated, finished with.

But there are moments of (clickety) sunlight
as a train leaves one tunnel
and enters the darkness of another (click).

She meant: to be there, just another of them,
with them, we bruise so easily, we are not alone, we are
    given back
to each other, we are loved, so let us be loved.

How else could she willingly get there? How strange
a friend from long before should stand on the platform
(and her door suddenly open) to ask, "*Wozu fährst du,*
    Edith, wozu?"

(Naked)
So that naked, however at ease, is terrible also
with the belly soft white, the veins just under
as blue threads crinkling, and the rise/fall ever so

gentle and exposed, and like a grub upturned,
a hermit-crab pulled out; and how quickly
hands, even with men, move to shield, care.

In women this is where embryos, curled, lie.
But how it can clench, ripple, slop before
– yes before– you notice the terrible cause,

a blade whirring, a jagged cry.
And, however spirited in well-being, how sometimes
you stare at yourself in the mirror, a corpse standing

eating the air. Although imagination refuses
to imagine yourself dead (yet?). Even if the body,
spindly survivor, knows its colours cold and bruised,

still you can only glance at photos
of bodies stacked, loosely splayed,
who no longer feel how cold they are.

Even when turning yourself under the shower nozzle
to sluice, hawk, clean under the loveliness of water
and relish the strength belly can release, but know too

this rots first later, we gas ourselves, how we drown
in ourselves, the way bodies flounder in Rousseau's painting
with overhead the horse and rider of final pestilence.

The Demoniac Later

There were two of us, and both of them were me,
    each with his own no-life;
sometimes king-of-the-castle, beggar-man, thief:
    Legion is a dangerous game to play;
sucking my flesh for hours, nibbling the hairs on my forearm,
    I was the sty where Legion lay.
Naked as a dead man and almost as at home,
    we dwelt among the tombs,
their chalk taste always on the tongue, and about us
    the dazzling whiff
    of something stale;
visitors are few, and have their own troubles,
    at worst will chuck a stone;
you can scrounge survival from pigs' left-overs.
    Even now my fists clench
as I recall how a savage sun could goad
    each of me to bite the other;
neither wanted to be healed. Lapping a rainpool once
    I saw what should have been my face
settle into a calmer, suffering face that was neither of us:
    he said "Legion is your name;
see your wound and be healed", forbade me to lick his hand,
    knowing we only half-want to be healed,
and made me stand and know myself
    to be sheer sunlight
and squalls of rain, can be deepest midnight
    but only to be noon.

The worst death is over. Gadara is a state of mind.
    Before returning to his home,
he taught me I can walk over the waters of all I was/we were,
    but he bade me wait
and tell whoever asked what I was who I am.
    The desert is the proper place for waiting,
here nothing happens and does not happen;
    the locals speak of me
as something like a man or as a joke.
    When I strip for bathing
I see a man bears the scars of healing;
    fish, bread, bitter herbs and wine
and a cupped hand of water are my food, my drink;
    avoiding the usual speeches, if I preach,
I preach only to myself, and murmur my unfaithful prayers.
    A man's story
is and is not greater than himself. Galilee is a state of mind.
    When I see the other demoniacs
I say, "There, but for the grace of God, go I"
    and then learn again to say, strangely,
"There, with the grace of God, go I."

Emphasis

As black on white,
or white on black imposes,
all speech is exaggeration;

except poetry: that curving line
surrounded by the silence
it encloses.

Sermon to the Birds

This was Brother Human speaking, but first he whistled
us down from the air to congregate in the dust.
A flutter of dismay as he announced his text:
on the death of sparrows. I live on crumbs myself
he said and I too am dying. Do not fear
if in a starving winter you fall from the heavens
above Assisi: for has not the Lord numbered
each of your feathers? *Pause.*
                    Your brother Chanticleer
alone of all creation raised his voice three times
against the darkest deed. The Lord remembers this.
Pause.
    Even you, my brothers, had your nests for comfort
when the Lord of All was spreadeagled on the cross. *Pause.*

Forgive my threadbare words. Pause breaks into twitters.

He tries Brother Sparrows, love Brother Starlings.
Now some took off, until one larrikin piped up:
how come the God of love who, so you say, makes us
makes the sparrow-hawk as well?
                            He had no answer
and stood there useless as a scarecrow, hands upraised.
So we perched on him, and pecked the hand-out grain.
The wounds in his palms twitched. At our squabbles over food
and sex he tut-tutted with a sad smile. The pious
stole threads from his gown. We all left him and flew off.

Speak, Lazarus

Lazarus awake, in stirring dark
and cold – ice-hard bones within face;
inward wisp of air, warm outward fall,
slight chill tug, slight gust pushed out.

    A sound lingers, like a breath, in the rock

– drowsy, in black echoes, skin prickles;
hand bound close over breast senses
slow thump within; air stinks of decay.

    Again, a voice speaks in syllables of stone

– a sudden tide of warmth melts through limbs,
veins and muscles thaw, and tongue moistens.

    The voice of a friend enlivens the air

gently,
with daring he moves a hand
to know the quick heart reverberating;
they're prising the rock; as his body stirs
flesh has the tang of herbs, or salt;
despite shafts of brightness and buds of noise,
he turns to that voice strongly calling

    Lazarus, Lazarus come out

– he breaks the larval binding cloths
and raises the fingertips
to touch the feeling petals of the lips;
to rise, buoyant in the tangle of the shroud,

he flexes himself, each pore open to the light;
a man held in the rapture of the sun,
he stands: blood like honey in the veins,
hived sunlight, with the pulse of fire resounding;
edging his way to the calling voice,
he learns again the exertion of walking;
outside the tomb

      in voiceless tears, my sisters;
a flight of parakeets scatters overhead
the troubled silent crowd; it is the Lord!
I thought there would be light, and only light;
Is this heaven, or earth? A fly settles
on my skin, a lizard scurries over a rock;
Is it the Lord, or I, who weeps?
      Lazarus, my brother, speak only
of the exertion of breathing, and the gift
of blood bright as honey in the veins.
Speak, Lazarus, to the murmurs of the crowd.

– stirring in the dark and cold, I heard a voice,
like yours, through the breathing rock, cry, "Awake
Brother Lazarus", so I arose and came,
words like salt or herbs on my lips,
and ready now to live and die a second time.

The Seals

Two human lovers watch the seals,
bull and cow, in the evening pool.

Each is the spiralling axis
around which the other turns.

As she coils/uncoils about him,
his great bulk overshadows her.

Enticing him, she breaks away
and sharply barks in playful fear,

but patiently he nudges her
towards his strong desire.

Again she whirls apart to provoke
his gentle yet sudden assault.

Enfolding her, he holds her now
in their rapture of the deep.

They rest on each other, adrift
in the current of their own making,

and reveal to human lovers
the gentleness of beasts.

Masters of Divinity

An ordinary Melbourne evening,
early rush hour, and the tram almost full;
clasping my parcels, and standing, footsore,
as we rattle homebound out of the city,
I hear your words, Lancelot Andrewes:
"*day cometh, and night cometh,
and cometh death, the living death.*"
For days, unnoticed, your voice has been with me,
but as it echoes, and dusk edges in,
all things now are tender to me: three girls
chat about books overdue, or home troubles,
and "Who is Andrew Marvell?" A woman
casually scratches her knee; another knits;
people glance at each other's magazines,
one man fends off intruders with a glare;
pressed close, human contact stays tentative
(a tram's a fine and private place,
and few, I think, do here embrace),
though a young man turns to smile at his girl,
and they try to be at home with each other.
The tram almost gives the rhythm of your speech,
Lancelot Andrewes, and rattles loudly
what's hidden in every human breath:
"*day cometh, and night cometh,
and cometh death.*"
      John Keats, near death in Rome, sent his friend
searching for Jeremy Taylor's mighty work
Holy Living and Holy Dying;

but since that book of melancholic prose
was nowhere found, the poet died alone
without the comfort of divinity;
to the friend, who held him in his arms,
he said at the end, "Don't breathe on me, Severn,
it comes like ice." Even a friend's loving breath
the best of us can find a living death.
      Nudging my way to the door, I half-hum
"day cometh, night cometh". Ahead of me
a student strums the handrail like a cello.
We'll get off, and all these faces will vanish
quick as names writ on water. Night moves in.
The chill air resounding with its clangour,
the tram trundles my fellow-passengers
down the avenue of darkening trees.
      Even those who have full mastery of speech
do no more than point toward the silence;
the rest of us, if lessoned by their words,
take our human frailty as a gift,
and so learn that only the skills of gentleness
and tender humour, fumble them as we do,
can meet the dark. In silence, your voice:
"Remember we to outstrip the night,
doing some good thing." More words of yours.
Holding them, I'll hobble homeward through the dark,
and name now all my brethren on the tram,
and even poets, both living and dead,
as masters of divinity.

Lancelot Andrewes, I know your voice,
and still seek my own.

The Ten Holy Saints of Hartland

St Andrew of Harton

Care for small creatures is my task,
those that scurry as I lift stones
to bid them well, that live in crevices
and innermost leaves. I can breathe
on deadish things and they live a little.

Mice, sparrows, slaters, lizards,
snails, and creatures with no easy name,
these war on each other and themselves.
Some know my whistle.

I am a small creature myself:
the vast heave of these hills
and whatever the sky is tell me so.

Hush while I tell you

Hush while I tell you.
This place is rich in saints,
if nothing else, as if
each century and hamlet had its own,
as if ordinary space could be holy.
Each saint once had a chapel
but now they stand in the reredos,
gathered as the glory of this church.

There's St Martin of Meddon, which no map shows,
but I'll tell you he was a leper up on moorland
and his disease made him holy, not inevitably.
St Wenn, of unknown sex, of Cheristow,
a visionary of the last times, and with local detail,
most terrible of all. Poor St Andrew of Harton,
famed for his whistling if nothing else.
St James of Milford and Higher Velly,
a travelling man and useful,
who knew the sea but died of landsman's violence.
St Clare of Phylham, whose needlework is all lost,
visitors came to watch her silence. And that just man,
St Leonard of Newton, and his many many children,
none of them his. It's a weary walk to Longfurlong,
and nothing to see, now nor ever:
that's why St John of the same name
chose it or it chose him.
Unlike St Catherine's Tor and Oratory,
still with its ancient tile and glass.
Maybe each of them is just a place
and the landscape has the quality of their holiness.

Of St Nectan there is much to say:
his is the great church here at Hartland
and there's another, most ancient of all, nearby
at Welcombe. From his tower on a clear day
you can see the southern downs of Wales
whence he came; his statue looks firmly into Devon.
He is our local glory; his deeds and prayers sustain the land
and warn for centuries against our cliffs and seas.

The Blessed Virgin of Fire Beacon tells you
that the Mother of us All is also a local.
Maybe you will hear their voices in the rain.
The great storms are comminations upon us;
we are chidden by where we live. We are blessed
by the rustling of leaves. Do not affront our sky.

St Clare of Phylham
Within this bowl the cosmos: a blue whorl,
a white aureole; how it fits in my hand,
or shows in negative cross-section of bone;
how the potter's finger-tip ridged the outside,
glazed with cornflower sky; a minor work.
Hold its simplicity, its care, with all your strength.
Look at the light-thread on the rim.

St Leonard of Newton
The live carved faces of the saved
stare across/down
the waters of the zigzag lake
(baptismal Gennesareth)
to the stony damned.

So I say:
Beware the proclaimed centre with its beguiling lie.
Find the crux by journeying to the edge.
Search out the numinous hamlets.
Discern with care the noises of animals.
And do your praying in a side aisle.

Our Lady, St Mary, of Fire Beacon
Homeward to Hartland
wayfarer over sea tracks,
landsman along cowpath.

Make her simple yes a beacon,
her desire to be folded in God's-will
inflame you with that infolding flame,
and so light your way with light your way.

The earth those days was dying too,
the sun did die, and withered nature
made its cry: "He bowed his head
and said not a mumbling word."
She watched, she stood the deadlong day.

See how she is a cruet of fire
raised into the dark, and yet
her yes is dangerous, her love
cruel to her, as if she torched herself.

These sights, traveller, will bring you home,
singing *"Kyrie"* all the way, *"eleison"* all the way.

St John of Longfurlong: His Two Showings
1
Now the spine's a mainmast,
come up in the crow's nest, Captain,
and meet the sky.

I'm swaying slightly, and feel the tug
on all my cordage, sense the shifts
in all my timbers. Mine eyes telescope
to see spouting at sea's horizon
Leviathan. Although our currents intermingle,
I leave him be, and he me. Yoga
(and more) does it.

2
Although I want a body
like a god's; my god's body
is this battered frailty
that on the cross I see.

St Catherine of Kernstone
From my high tor I'll say winter
is the time for coming here.

Leave the village on the downward westward road:
you'll glimpse the tower with its four pinnacles
over high hedges, bare trees. Note
early greys and brown reds,
and water trickles trickles in roadside trenches;
the whirr of a saw, the common cries of gulls,
even a few unknown December flowers, the sky
a broad watercolour wash, the church gone.
The walk is long and easy, everything sweetly sodden.
(Be alert to sounds, you notice.)

The combes lightly darkly wooded,
the air almost lightest rain.
The tower will rise again, with the statue in a niche
facing eastward centuries
of parishioners, occasional pilgrims,
decades of trippers, church-crawlers.
(Let your heart sing this purposeful stroll.)
Repeatedly St Nectan's tower rises up
a dark light-house.

St Martin of Meddon

Hartland is the highest edge
of England. That is why they come
from the ends of the earth,
pilgrims to a pun
and paradox. Nearby
is a place called Welcombe.

The hart is most sensitive of beasts:
Dearheart is Christ: our heartland too:
which cost him dear: edged out he was:
to centre us: take heart, he bids us welcome.

An Angel Blows Its Own Trumpet

I will not say, "Do not be afraid".
You have much to fear. You are common folk
and this is merely England. I have spoken

to the wild sages of the desert and the holy monks
of Cappadocia, shimmered in the mosaics of Byzantium,
tiptoed late summer afternoons across pink floors
to whisper messages to the saints of Umbria.

You will mistake my trumpet for a fox's bark.
Indeed this is night-time. Nevertheless,
I remind you that out of darkness light will rise
like a tower. Meanwhile you have much to suffer
and the only alleviation will come from the promise of light.
For more, you have the Scriptures. I also play the viol,
which signifes the life everlasting, but too sweetly high
for your ears to hear. So be afraid.

St James of Milford and Higher Velly

First I saw an eagle passing through great water.

Second I saw a vine, which the great dragon did bite,
myself a leaf only.

               Third I saw with her chicks
the pelican in piety, which means redemption.

Fourth, and trampling on a serpent,
a hart, lord of a green hill.

Again I saw, and saw an angel stooped to light
upon Nectan's tower and to cry like a trumpet,
"This is hart's land." Therefore, obey its green.

St Wenn of Cheristow

In my dream I saw how
St Nectan's took to fire,
centuries of slow accretions,
storage, care, go up.

Fire tracery removes all tracery of wood,
the rot of England sets its sweetness all alight,
the palaces burn, fire-power falls on itself,
the silly imperial throne subsides in ash.

How flames grapple, scamper, leap from
beam to beam. I saw
the nave rafters take, I saw
the shingles ablaze, the stones crack.

The church became the fire beacon
no one sees. I live
under the upturned nave
of a wrecked boat.

The Silence of St Nectan of Hartland and Welcombe

As you move away,
glance back/up at Nectan's statue.
Nectan does not speak.
Unless the stern Atlantic force high
about our cliffs,
across the russet moorland
and into the rustling

leaves of the dark-bedded combes
is his speech. Unless
his tower builds itself flinty
into the stern wind as his song,
and the nave that springs from its power
carries his echo.

Stone arches over the dead
and witnesses what becomes of them.
The presence you sense
(comforting/challenging)
is what the saint of this place
says to you. You need nothing else.

Thank You for Your Visit
The locals will not thank you
for thinking this a back-water.
Here is what history is for,
and this church has hallowed it.
So that the oddity of the Emperor Haile Selaisse's chair,
used for his odd visit in 1938, is forgiven,
and one wonders how he felt, welcomed by Devon
courtesy and accents. Surreal facts:

the present church built circa 1360,
interior high and spacious,
filled with pale colour: blue, white, gold, terracotta, green;
richly carved Norman font,
Jacobean pulpit with Renaissance panels,

the second highest tower in this county,
above the north porch the Pope's Chamber,
the rood screen the largest if not the longest hereabouts,
note the eleven bosses of the North Aisle: the hart
(which is Christ) tramples the serpent Satan.
Hugh Prust of Thorny at his own expense in 1540
paid for all the seats in North Chancel aisle.
The lumber and devices of holy history are stashed here.

Please remember this is a place of prayer,
you may wish to make a donation for roof repair,
leave something here. You may take a switch of hazel
to smuggle back to wherever you came from,
at the bus-stop the pottery offers a choice of momentos,
we recommend the small blue bowls.
Thank you for your visit,
but go.

Mousepoem
Morsels of Divinity

God is the moon
unending cheese
>   on moonfilled nights
>   we can be caught worshipping,
>   dozens of us still in the open
>   entranced by that cold beauty

his phases confuse us:
our sects are Waxers and Waners,
our doubters declare
>   the moon is dead
>   or it's merely a cold disturbance in the sky,

our theologians define him as
>   ancona, caciocavallo, cotrone, fontine d'aosta,
>   formaggio dolce, gorgonzola, grana (parmesan
>   or reggian), iglesias, leonessa, mozzarella,
>   cacio pecorino romano, pecorino dolce, pimento,
>   puglia, robbiole, sapsago, viterbo,
>   bellunese, emmentaler, petit suisse, thraanen,
>   bondon, brie, briol, coulommiers, morin,
>   neufchâtel, petit carré, port du salut,
>   saint-michel, septmoncel, tête-de-maure,
>   gex, herve, limburger,
>   algau, backstein, carinthian, emmersdorf,
>   glarner-, grüner-, kräuter-käse, grottenhof,
>   ihlefeld, lindenhoff, malakoff, manbollen,
>   marianhof, schabziger, schützen, tanzenberg,
>   thuringia caraway, caerphilly, cheddar, cheshire (possibly),

   lanark, stilton, wensleydale,
   oka, livlander, and perhaps bombala blue,
   but not katzenkopf
   and never rat-trap,
and the true believer says
   "all of us are really lunatic
   and the hidden side of him
   is paradise"
our visionaries have seen the dead
   scurrying through the Vale of Roquefort
   and scrambling over the Mountains of Gruyère;
   yes, we'll sail on dry biscuits
   across the Seas of Camembert,
   and we'll reach at last our blue-veined home,
   the Garden of Edam!
there, our song, our dance, will be:
"You are cheese unending
the cheese of cheeses
God is Gouda!"

How the Ocean Is Undermined

Look how they hold steady
fathoms down; they've risen
from so much deeper, but won't
surface, don't want to abandon
their little golden fish;

or: words will not undrown
themselves
from suffused blue sound;

or: red poems
suspend themselves
in sonar energy —
touch
their fishy bulk
goes BOOM!

Exuberance of a Blind Infanta

Two ravens eye the eyes
of the blinded infanta.

To her mastiff, she sings
"Oranges taste of orange";

to her dwarf, she whispers
aloud "Barefoot certainties

of earth, of hot Andaluz,
urge me to hop, to dance";

to herself: "I live alone
in a tarpaulin shroud:

peck my canvas, songless birds.
O bittersweet is Andalucia."

Interior Palomar

Waiting for
interior Palomar
to open and perceive
the exuberant spray of spray.

Waiting for
the Temple hinges
to swing and reveal
ordinary children
at their ancient games.

Waiting for
sudden bells to make
an unattended sky
attended blue.

Pity the Rich

Pity the rich
in their dark-glassed cars
who have only
what they own,
know too little
about possession
and have disinherited
themselves from the earth:
they will be with us always.

Friday 3.30*

Friday three-thirty.
The soldiers have packed up and gone.

The other corpses do not have your quiet.
We share the silence. This is how we speak.

The task is finished.
Only the flies have anything to do.

You kept your word unbroken.

Below, in the city,
they follow the ancient cycles.

I should have been here earlier.
You are grateful I came at all.

Bells toll nowhere.

You are the most secret man.

They bring your mother. The rites begin.

All this, somehow, was inevitable.

Your quiet fills the world.
The new time is poised
to break upon us all.

Naked Runner

The women, Peter and the beloved disciple
  were the foremost, but you, latecomer, are the one
I am waiting for. Do not be amazed
  at the unearthly brightness of my presence,
and do not wonder about the stone rolled back,
  though that is what has brought you here.
Wonder, rather, that except for ourselves this tomb
  is empty, the linen is folded: here he lay
briefly during our harrowing hours of aftermath.
  Already the story is being told in various ways
and already countered: you will hear plausible rumours
  about a theft; you yourself will falter
over your own story. Here is another, the same as any:
  Imagine a young man, who from childhood foamed
with violence. He was drowning in fire. Healers quailed
  as their gifts failed. Until, to drive out such darkness
with a quick prayer, the Master came. Afterwards
  the healed man kept near him, as if in a childhood garden
scented with happiness, even when in this holy city
  threats circled around the Master and his followers.
Even when distant shouts of soldiers drew the young man
  from bed;
  clad only in a linen cloth, and their lights showed the way
to the garden where darkness itself came for all he loved,
  the young man did not flee. Until no miracle happened.
Only the Master understood, but the followers were swamped/
  scorched by fear. Each was drowning in darkness.

A soldier lunged at the young man, who ran away naked.
    I was that naked runner.
I am surprised as you are to find the story
    of one's own disaster changed by the unearthly brightness
which the Master's story now brings to mine. As if to be naked
    is to be close to the truth, but I ran away. And yet
in the long night blundered to this empty, surprising place,
    which was waiting.
We, who were worse than we supposed, now find ourselves
    more than we ever dreamed. Do not try to understand,
though now you must try your story in a new way.
    Notice the scent of lavender. Go back to the beginning,
which is Galilee. If you meet a gardener, speak to him.

Mobypoems

Ahab's Songs

1.
Call me Ahab.
The great whale it is
that seeks me. The sea's
full of Moby, all awash with him.
Moby's underwater thunder
– take soundings of his quiet.
Moby's the only nuggetty thing there:
he's the most nuggetty thing anywhere,
is Moby. Hear white thunder below there.
Call it nautical lingo.

2.
I'm counting the seas: the sea I'm upon
– it's underkeel – is "one", it's beyond fathoming,
it's Moby's shifting habitat.

The thunder-sea's above – that's "two",
and it comes in rainstorm; a black-white cloud
can be a whale; beware lightning flukes.

Which is hell? you're asking;
both, brother, and the air between.
All this weather's on deck, I bring it with me.

Maybe land- and heavenly-weather too.
Ashore, my wound makes me lurch and roll;
I'm a seafarer, where the boat and all is lurch and roll.

The Pequod limps afloat. It's my craft.
I've seen the sky twang with heat, with song.
Moby lives in the first ocean.

3.
Is Moby God? you're wondering.
I'll answer you from my researches
in and across the deeps: almost, brother.
It's enough to know that he outsizes us.

Do not think my name is Ahab only,
nor that Moby is the other's name;
this is not the Pequod neither,
nor out from Nantucket nor Manila Bay.

My craft is like the sea,
myself, the white creature,
(if creature is what Moby is): we're all
nameless, empty, shining.

4.
Here comes Ahab, they say, be wary.
Something ate his leg, chomp, chomp
went his destiny, fate or happenstance, was it?
A whale's tooth's a mighty thing.

Mostly I keep to my cabin,
apart from me nothing's there.
Worse, they murmur, I keep to my hurt heart,
apart from me nothing's there.

Soon I'll give you shanties, and in scrimshaw.
My craft's all harpoons and tackle.

Let's put to sea. Beware of Ahab,
he'll bite you: the bitten bite hard.

5.
Let me tell you the leg-story,
since you do not ask.
I remember nothing; but awoke
to know the whale had eaten me.

What's left of me is a phantom's pains:
I am not here. Whatever it was
assailed me was sudden,
surgical, and for my own good.

The alternative I was told
and tell myself was worse.
There's less pain than you suppose.
I walk on one live, one dead.

That's the leg-story.

6.
Moby's eaten me. I'm not Jonah.
Mine's a bitter/better tale.
What's gone of me is gone.

Through my scars, I eye the world;
through my wounds gape Moby's eyes.
Maybe the sea's aweeping immeasurable tears.

My body's that of a ruined god;
it can get no better/worse.
Remember how Jesus' side took the harpoon.

Jonah rose again out of whalebelly;
I stomp about on whalebone.
What's left of me's left over.

Moby and I, we have a mutuality:
a hatred gives a life a purpose.
Do not call Moby Jesus, nor Jesus Moby.

7.
Here's Ahab imagining he's overboard,
plunging Mobywards, and Moby's spiralling
with Ahab lashed on board him. The shining
deeps resonate with his hooting song.

Whatever's to horror at, flounder in,
Moby revels in. He plummets Ahab
into the pit of darkest water. Drown me,
Moby, before you mangle me again.

The sea is God's doing, and Moby maybe.
Together they'll work so Ahab's mind's,
heart's, all of me's, engulfed
and done for.

8.
I cannot force the whale
out of the deep, so wait
stumping around the deck.

He'll come, though, again,
breach his element into mine,
and make mayhem here.

There'll be many more deaths
before Moby's done adrowning.
Watch for white underwater shadows.

Moby's a cloud, a sail, a sheet,
a shroud, a blank.

9.
Moby poises such strength
in the flukes of him,
there'll be such upsurge of him;
his pale blue eyes eye
the shadow of my hull.

10.
Let's consider the making of Moby.
An act of love was it, to form a thing
so vast and cruel, so much itself?
Yes, there's majesty in the flukes of him,
there's wonder at the arc of his breaching,
at the thudding spray as his bulk
curves to go under. He flicks our craft
with his flukes and munches our limbs
and companions. Even when his albino presence
is not there. How can the sea be hallowed
with Moby in it? Is not the whale-maker accountable
for the whale's deeds? I finger my scar
from inside me. God is the greatest wound.

11.
I have never known woman,
and the sea I'm bitter at:

I gave it my life, and the sea
— for all its sweet breezes and swaying currents —
took it, with my blood and gristle and beauty.

I've sent the killer-boats
to water-beetle across the pacific surface.
The crews believe they're hunting Moby;
they're my decoys — they'll lure him to my element.
Moby and I, we're each other's prey.

The harpoons that glance off his sheer side
hit the waters that conspire with Moby.
I'll wound the sea, watch it heave with pain.
Moby'll rise again like an upsurging berg,
the shimmering scree of him upend my craft.

Moby, I'm singing, come to me.
Gnaw your way through the deep.
Show your facelessness.
Here's more of me for you.

12.
I'm underwater myself, drowned, adrift
and looking way up there at the silver undersurface.
look there, floating downward, so stately,
comes my craft — stove in by Moby.

This is my lament for how the great timbers gave
— that white blankness thudded the bow away;
all crew, all tackle, my mainmast shattered,
the barrels and barrels of light-shining spermaceti

rolled and dragged adown the slimy sea.
All that cargo – the men's manhood – I saw sink
past me. All lingo tumbling into the nothing sea.
All my cargo's gone.

I'm mourning the Pequod/Atlantis
– the whiteness made a vortex for,
sucked us under. All my craft and cargo's gone.
– grammar, words, names, sounds going …

13.
Now I'm Moby's song.
The deep rings with what he's done
to me; he bears my wounds
upon his back; his whiteness
runs with my bloody gristle;
my killing is the sonar tale
he tells through the mighty currents;
my loss his flukes thwack
across the stunned/attentive seas.
Moby's singing is all of me.

Ishmael's Shanties

1.
Do not call me Ishmael,
although I'm the survivor
who tells the tale – I'm the narrator –
of how I alone escaped to tell you.

What happened stranded me.
There are statistics:
– this is not in Scripture –
of the fifteen of us afflicted alike

over ten years, I alone escaped.
We were too young to be chosen,
– and only males were taken;
from three untold million,

I alone am spared to tell you
that I have fourteen nameless companions.
One I saw, cheery as he was whited out:
cheerio, brother, I alone was saved to say.

Now I sense God's amazement
at what befell, at what befalls.
I am Job's messenger perhaps,
or call me instead, Isaac.

2.
We're all Queequeg-like
worshipping our false prick-god;
our stories are hidden-tattooed
on our bodies: our bodies tell
how we are towards the gods.
Queequeg, brother, I float alive
on your empty coffin.

3.
How in the try-works barrels
we waded hip-high
in the sea of spermaceti:

we strode in those slight-tugging
tangles of light, singing manly shanties;
with full-throated ease we slowly died.

4.
When I am a child, I dolphin in the sea,
my tiny flukes play with the deeps,
the air is clean, the sea is sweet,
I float and frolic on such immensities.

5.
I beheld the vast white shape
of Moby surge out of the deep:
his only feature was his blue-pink stare.

As he bent himself downwards again
he raised aloft on spread-eagled flukes
Ahab, crucified: Jesus crucified on his Father.

So we on ours.
Those flukes were withdrawn underwater
and Ahab harrowed into the deeps.

The gulls swooped over the calming whirlpool
crying behold, behold,
and I alone escaped to tell you.

Queequeg's Prayers

1.
Let me/Queequeg pray, now I'm drowned,
and he (Ishmael) floats in air
on my coffin: he hugs it,
hugging a lost father found.

I'm humming/hymning to myself
– he's holding him: now he's saved –
I'm floating too, downward, bubble bubble
- farewell brother, prays me/Queequeg.

My coffin did not save me,
my corpse is all I have
– phosphorescent putrescence –
I sing myself holy wholly holey.

2.
My skin all over is inked
with who, where, whence, whereto
is me, my stories, homeland-and-sea.
Call me/Queequeg, here's me –
skin, flesh, bones, name, voice, my tale.
Fishes scrutinise my parchment,
mouth at my beginnings/ends,
tickle the heavens – star beasts
are all over me. Translate me, would you?
Hidden lingo tattoos
my skin cosmos. (To make a man
the elders with inky fish teeth
bites traced sky/earth/sea into/onto me.)
Search, little fishes, the password into me
with your tiny teeth. My scars too,
all those cicatrices, criss-cross me
with stories. Decipher me/Queequeg.

3.
When I was a child
>   the sea tried to gobble
>   me up/down.

From panicking air
>   a dark man kindly
>   snatched/saved me.

My second life's done,
>   the sea eats away
>   my story:

it began once
>   upon a time I lived
>   happily

ever after, but
>   now I am a man -
>   where's Daddy?

lift me shoulder high,
>   tell me to be – bird
>   beast – fish – child –

king – a harpooner –
>   a harpoon – a whale
>   Moby white.

4.
O look way down there the Pequod's flanks
crack inwards, its barrels of spermy light
explode, look there, way beneath those nebulae, look
Moby's maggotty bulk, his flukes tattooed with Ahab.

How I arose in the bow of the chase boat
to balance and coil my skill to lunge into Moby
mine own harpoon, how we bloodied him and he us,
I scarred him – my mark on Moby, Moby's on me/Queequeg.

5.
I'm upright fathoms down
hoisted deepwards, I finger akimbo side-currents,
the sea lowers me, gently does it.

They're singing in my earholes, the little fishes,
they wriggle their way through all my gaps,
they gush into my mouth-gape, tingle through my bowels.

Run, run, little fishes, do the sea's bidding.

I'm maggotty white, they nibble off bits
/bites of me, I'm crumbing away,
I'm losing myself morsel by morsel.

A shark has nosed me – soon it'll razor –
I'll be ahabed all away,
these creatures are Moby's maybe angels.

Prey, the little fishes, on me/Queequeg.

That is my body shoaling away from me
in silvery flashes, I'm shredding away
into a coil of bubbles, upward I/they go.
This is some prayer I'm praying brother,
bit by bite I nourish the ocean,
what's left is mumbo-jumbo, amen-talk:

   Pity, all ye sea beasts, him/Ahab, praise him/Moby.

They're tugging my mouth away,
I'm scattering bread crumbs, they take and eat,
brotherself farewell, I'm becoming sea, so be it.

Laguna de Bay

The world is full of world.
There is no flatness in it.
Even the desert plain bends
in the light and, night-time,
fills up with space.

At Laguna de Bay
I saw a lake within a lake,
and a downpour pour down
vertical ocean.
Who has not seen pools of sunlight
on the sea?
Or heard, heavy on the roof, the rain
applaud itself?
Or watched leaves sweat green
and out come the lizards
lovely and lithe and tiny and vanish?

The moon, too, is full of world:
watching it makes you brimful.

The Buddha of the Southern Ocean
for Don and Anna, in thanks

Today, returning to my exercise,
    above the beach, not quite alone,
yoga-like, I touched the earth
    with hands, foot, torso; in a slight sweat
my body found itself, gesture by gesture.
    Only afterwards did I realise
the Buddha at Don's place yesterday
    had a leg missing too (who knows the story?).
The right hand rested over the remaining knee
    in the "touching-the-earth" attitude,
the other lay cupped above the missing thigh.
    "Look at the straightness of the back, so balanced,
the closed eyes, his smile, so serene."
    The Buddha sits on the kitchen window-sill,
traces of gilt sparkle on the firm torso;
    the rainforest and mist rise up behind him.
Nearby: utensils, flowers in a vase,
    bags of food, bottles, a handbag.
Anna's burnished-grey whippet tiptoes
    around the airy room. The Buddha
blesses everything and nothing.
    "I am the Buddha of the Southern Ocean."

Bodhisattva

1.
Forgive my serenity.
With all my hands I return to you.
Take my gestures for comfort: so
I ward off your fears, proffer charity,
pray for you. With another mudra
I touch the earth and its demons are stilled.
Touch the earth with your own hand.
Be saved and save. Leave me.

2.
My palm reveals all-seeing blessings.
This is the courtesy of heaven.

Know: you have your own smile, sudden, subtle,
and your own nimbus: laughter.
These are the treasures of earth.

Stone
*Document of Land Purchase from Earth Spirits
Korea: Koryo Period, 1143 AD*

1.
In your land, Earth Spirits,
we bury our dead.

Let this stone witness
your kindness to the dead.

Already you know them;
soon we will meet you.

Yes, we speak too much;
you do not speak at all.

A king would use gold words
on immortal jade.

These words will vanish;
the stone, though, will endure.

We have used stone
to remind ourselves for ever.

2.
This is where I bury my father.
Be kind to him, Earth Spirits.

This tablet is my homage to you.
In stone I bow for ever.

Earth

How the first time
the engines roared and forced
along the runway,
all my back pushed
itself into the backrest.
My body, decades on,
thrills to remember.
I learnt to trust the earth
(its machines)
while leaving it.

Whingeing Poems

1.
God and me, we've gone quiet on each other.
Master (I do not say) here is my complaint:
this world's your doing (not mine); your gravity
hard/sharp crashes me down, O Lord of all.

I cannot live here safely, my body's always quailing
from always falling. I've been mugged, Sir,
by your creation, and there's still harder doing I'm yet
to be done by – there's your knock out/down blow.

Sweet my Lord, you're here with me I know,
have contusions of your own I see, got
by reaching for me here on your hard hard ground.
With your own crutch, prop me upwards I pray.
Sir, there's too much talk of suffering, let's just do it
and go. Meanwhile, I'm still not talking.

2.
Greetings, Master, and here is my complaint:
your plan, if that's the word, is unstuck.
Hurt is hurt is hurt and little more.
What's more you're hurting too. All's un/done for.

If somehow hope's in it, how
is not for me to say, and you're not telling either.
So there you are, and I am/we are, so there.
At best it can be said my/our mess is yours.

Yes, we're tiresome: we're tired out.
We're trying to get used to this place:
somehow it suits us, how we know all too well.
It's a kind of comfort to have you here.
Darkness, Sir, covers your earth.
At least you're here to see it. So here you/we are

3.
Thank you for not answering
my prayer: death is one's own size,
oneself's a tiny burden.
You give me your terrible peace,
And there must be reverence.

Brother Waldmann's Last Carving*†

See the tower, dark silo, raise itself
into moonlit moonlight.
Hear the vines labour through the night to hoist
earth's sweetness into store.
Know wine, grapes' exuberance gathered,
become a dark harvest.
Night wind, a glory, surges over hills
to brunt about his stonework.

Praise how, old, blind, the carver skills the stone
into leaf and grape to adorn a door.
Chip by chip, Brother Waldmann puts his mark,
tiny, intricate, on the vast smooth wall,
all his long night of reverent service,
while, aloft, the Southern Cross adorns a sky.

---

†Note: The capital of the left column to the main door of St Aloysius' Church, Sevenhill, was carved by Brother Waldmann SJ after he had gone blind.

Part 2

New Poems

The Romans

The Romans, to give them credit,
organised how to kill with maximum effect.
To kill a man, pitch him between spread arms/hands
so they take his full weight, until exhaustion
makes him shift it to his legs, until
exhaustion makes him shift to hang on his hands/arms.
This can go on for days, as fear of stifling to death
keeps the shifting going. Sometimes as a mercy, more often
as an efficiency, they'd break the legs
so that death could get on with it.
They were strong in law, were the Romans,
so justified what they were doing,
and, good engineers, rarely botched the job.

Three Days

Friday

This Friday was no different from any other.
The usual criminals, after due process
somewhat bent, underwent the proscribed punishments:
torture, whatever degradation came their way, death.
The rabble roared and spat. Families and friends wailed
and went silent. The soldiers, I am glad to report,
did their duty and returned to barracks,
according to the Friday routine.

Offering

Father, we bring you the body of Jesus;
this is all we have; his blood is everywhere.
Sorry.

Saturday

Tomorrow is the third day.
Today is the day before, and the day after
what has numbed us. This is the day
when we have some chance of telling
what has happened so far – the catastrophe
and the jangling memory of the promise.
If tomorrow fulfils this, then we will be too full to speak,
as yesterday we were too empty.

Today, between times, if there is a between,
is the day for telling – to ourselves above all,
and to any who wish to overhear.   One of the promises was
that there were three days.

Sunday

The body of Jesus was pierced through and through
and through and through and through -
that's five, without counting those the thorns
made on his brow. He showed his risen wounds
on the days of the resurrection to tell us who he was
and that they were there for ever.

An Epistle to the Welsh

St Paul's letter to the Welsh, or at least to those in Llantwit,
has gone missing. Perhaps it is just as well.
He had not written to the rain before,
or to the slow driving wind, the draughts under the door,
the endless winter nights and brief damp-clogged days
– all of which prevent our hearing, huddle us around the fire
with just sparks of gossip or local feuds.
Maybe he spoke a poem to us instead,
which would have a better chance of huddling into us
– welcome as a piece of toast.
Certainly Paul preached on these church steps,
though all the scholars, even the holy ones, deny it.
Even so he had the rain to contend with.
If he taught us to praise the rain,
that would indeed have been new teaching, and welcome:
"The rain here, if you look closely, is green. Like Christ
     Our Lord."

Costa Rican Notes

A leaf trembles
on the trembling water
in a shifting bowl
upon a shifting table
on the quaking earth,
though all else is still;
and vice versa.

An azure kingfisher darts across
the azure sky unseen;
the greenest parrot
hides in the forest, scarlet
fruit its tiny head,
clinging to a branch with two yellow spiders.

The howler monkey vanishes
into its vast howl.

No volcanoes or insurrections here,
the mountain range maintains its democratic calm.
The quetzal is the national bird,
but makes far less of itself than it could.

Metaphysics/Grammar/Theology

A line so reticent
it is almost not there
reveals that there it is, just.

A line so frail
it trembles on the verge
reveals the spare authority of its presence.

What is there is other
and draws acknowledgement
(consider each absolute sparrow)
— to ignore it is the sin.

A subject singled out
receives a predicate
also singled out,
each from everything else.

I am thinking of a Sung Dynasty
Ding meiping vase
with a slightly slumped nozzle
and trickles of white glaze, perfect
as Jesus' risen wounds.

"Although it is raining, I will go to town."
"I will go to town, although it is raining."
The difference is in the suspense:
the play of expectation, satisfaction and surprise.
Literature springs from this.
In the above, the first is Augustan,
the second Romantic, maybe.

Sky-People
(for my father, whose workplace was the heavens)

The kingdom of heaven is like this, maybe,
fat chance, no way, thank God or the heavens.

In the Arrival/Departure lounge
people are having the best/worst time of their lives.
Arrival trolleys are piled high with too much luggage,
passengers wear the wrong clothes for the climate
and scan the crowd for a relative's smile or cry,
parents cope with a newly-bearded son, and his surprising
    Swedish girl,
aunties wave an Aussie flag, or foist a toy koala in your face;
you're here for the wedding/funeral,
or leaving for likewise.
You're so happy to be arriving/departing,
your neighbour's so sad.
The digital board rachets on
another load of arrivals/departures.

Although everywhere, even in the sky
God travels Economy:
way down the back near the mum with squalling children,
the refugee bits of family, or someone locked
onto the plain-clothed cop and escorted home for questioning.

Usually I don't declare that I'm "Father",
in case I get "Oh" or "Well, I have my own religion",
or my neighbor wants to be moved elsewhere,
or is a religious nutter and I'm trapped across the Pacific.

Sometimes, however, and rarely, the meeting
across the aisle can be sweetly fresh
and we're in the kingdom of heaven
until we have to land.

Qantas zeuses its way through the clouds,
its rivals merely icarus.
This is your captain speaking
in-flight information for onward passengers,
Qantas regrets the delay.

Despite gold-pink clouds suitable
for a sprawl of gods and goddesses,
there are no divinities up here;
now up/down is all relative,
there is no room for them to breathe:
heaven is absolute space, or nowhere.

With low white clouds coiling/uncoiling
here be dragons; gold filigree apsaras
finger the air; a flock of angels
swoop and pitch in formation;
or the clouds open to disclose
an azure message from the sky:
the earth has a halo,
everything has a halo.

Earlier we were flying over pink-gold
cordilleras of cloud, with sky-blue
lakes down there,
and then over soft cloud meadows
with a white sea beyond;

now tilting earthwards,
we're flying in white
tissue.

Only humans fly on hired wings –
to leave the earth before our time
is as solemn an undertaking
as listening to Bach.

Remember how at night the window view
showed all those fire-lights across India,
tracing the curvature of the earth,
and down there was humanity.

Prague

Easter Sunday after flying eastwards,
the bells make more sense than the language.

The coast of Bohemia is far inland,
and most of us are tourists here.

The palaces of the ancient regime
are renovated by the nouveau riche.

Here this happened and that happened;
here they invented and tested defenestration.

The paint on the newly opened church nearby
is barely dry; its little bell notes each quarter hour.

Small cars dart through cobbled streets
like cats. Newly-tiled roofs are orange.

This was home, indeed realm, of the Winter Queen,
a Stuart princess who did not stay long. This is Bohemia, Lady.

How did this room get through the War,
and its dour aftermath?

Various languages cross the little courtyard below, the police
move through in pairs: *Mitteleuropa*, plus tourists.

Nearby is the old Jewish Quarter.
There is nothing to be said.

I lean out of my new window
and am part of the scene.

Jewish Cemetery

Place a pebble of remembrance on a tombstone.
Outside the wall a blackbird sings its blackbird song:
"I'm a blackbird, be my mate, or move away."
The trees, budding their green, leaf to each other.
On the synagogue walls are names,
77,297 of them, with the date of birth if known,
and the date of deportation.
Small stones, names, a blackbird at its song.

Kestrel
for David Barron

Brother, all those years ago
when I caught the eye of the angel of death,
you were there to greet me again the next day.
There were others too whose faces
we've recognised in the school photo,
and recalled a few names, the wintry trees behind,
soon before we'd go our ways.

Let these memories brace me,
when again, like a kestrel,
the dark-feathered one eyes me again.

Sparrowpoems

1.
Who might be priested? Those with little to say
and say it briefly. Those who love bread.
Those who undertake a lifelong journey
into the mystery of their bodies.

Those who want for nothing.
Those who every day find the gospels
incomprehensible, who can find Jesus
among the poor, or nowhere.

Those who like to dirty their hands
with holy oils, and who notice
the fall of a sparrow and grieve for it.
Those who discover that placing oneself

in the presence of God takes a lifetime,
as does making a composition of place,
any place – where are we?
Those who can bless an open grave.

2.
On the Incarnation, for want of a better word.
How to be clumsy; how to be bruised.
When *Abba* Joseph died, how the sky disappeared,
until slowly the singing returned.
How to see what others don't: who notices the fall of
    a sparrow?

To relish the liveliness of visiting cousins:
a good joke on the Romans, others less so,
and yet more gossip on that family with two sons.
How it is time for another stint nightlong in the hills.
How the world is full of world, but of Satan too.

3.
A lament for sparrows; indeed where are they?
Time was a cheeky male, dark brown cap on his head,
shared with me the vast school hall, after the boys moved off:
a scratchy hopping sound, then a head cocked around the door,
crumb hunting in good crumb country
    (he looked at me and I at him)
until a human footfall sent him off.
Australia is no place for sparrows:
tiny convicts and until recently tough survivors,
minding their own business and on the make.
Brother Sparrow, where are you?

So Why Melbourne, Andy?

Close to the city centre
in the confines of the park,
the wild grasses are wild.
Their names are science or common,
the first recondite, and the common
vaguely known, but they grow
hip-high, profuse over the hillrise and beyond,
sweet smelling in gusts, in waves of blanched colours,
impenetrable even to dogs, here and there a stalk stands out.
Praise also the autonomy of nameless birds.

Born in Old South Wales, at the age of thirteen Andrew Bullen was diagnosed with cancer, resulting in the amputation of his right leg. His family moved to Australia in 1964 and he finished his schooling at the Jesuits' St Aloysius' College, Sydney, New South Wales. He joined the Jesuits in 1967.

Along with the usual priestly training he finished an Arts degree at Monash University followed by an MA that focused on religious poetry in Australia. He was ordained priest in 1979, and worked in teaching, chaplaincy and educating young Jesuits. He served two terms as assistant to the Jesuit provincial, edited the spirituality magazine *Madonna*, and currently is parish priest of Our Lady of the Way, North Sydney.

His interest in literature has found expression in his poetry. As well as literature, he finds inspiration in the everyday objects of religion – scripture, saints, places of pilgrimage and religious art and artefacts – and in his own experience.

Andrew writes about the strangeness of life and of the exigencies and blessings of living with a handicap. He sings of the gift of human frailty, by which we 'learn that only the skills of gentleness / and tender humour ... can meet the dark'. Humour is there aplenty, as well as loving observations of the everyday and of the exotic, and a delight in travel and in art.

He has a long-time interest in the visual arts and in 2010 was one of the three judges for the Blake Prize for Religious Art.

www.ingramcontent.com/pod-product-compliance
Lightning Source LLC
Chambersburg PA
CBHW031120080526
44587CB00011B/1047